# VOCAL SELECTIONS

Ken Davenport & Robyn Goodman

in association with

Walt Grossman    Ruth Hendel    Sharon Karmazin    Matt Murphy    Mark Shacket

present

Book by
## Kevin Del Aguila

Music and Lyrics by
## Gary Adler & Michael Patrick Walker

Conceived by **Marc Kessler & Ken Davenport**

Featuring

Ryan Duncan    **David Josefsberg**    Andy Karl

Tyler Maynard    Scott Porter

and

**Shadoe Stevens** as the voice of **G.O.D.**

| Set Design | Lighting Design | Costume Design |
|---|---|---|
| Anna Louizos | Natasha Katz | Gail Brassard |

| Sound Design | Vocal Arrangements | Orchestrations |
|---|---|---|
| Simon Matthews | Gary Adler & Michael Patrick Walker | Doug Katsaros & Lynne Shankel |

| Casting Director | Production Stage Manager | Hair Design | Production Manager |
|---|---|---|---|
| David Caparelliotis | Pat Sosnow | Josh Marquette | Andrew Cappelli |

| Associate Producer | Press Representatives | General Manager |
|---|---|---|
| Stephen Kocis | David Gersten & Associates | Roy Gabay |

Music Direction/Dance Music and Additional Arrangements
Lynne Shankel

Choreographed by
## Christopher Gattelli

Directed by
## Stafford Arima

Originally presented in the 2004 New York Musical Theatre Festival

Production photos courtesy of Carol Rosegg
Studio photo courtesy of SpotCo

ISBN-13: 978-1-4234-1969-3
ISBN-10: 1-4234-1969-3

WILLIAMSON MUSIC®

A RODGERS AND HAMMERSTEIN COMPANY

www.williamsonmusic.com

EXCLUSIVELY DISTRIBUTED BY

HAL•LEONARD®
CORPORATION

7777 W. BLUEMOUND RD. P.O. BOX 13819 MILWAUKEE, WI 53213

Visit Hal Leonard Online at
www.halleonard.com

## GARY ADLER

The son of a big-band trombonist and a girl-singer, Gary was born near Detroit, Michigan in 1965. He attended the University of Michigan in Ann Arbor, where he studied music composition with William Bolcom. He ultimately was awarded his Bachelor's Degree in Piano Performance, and became a pianist for the theatre.

Both on and off Broadway, Gary has played in the pits of *Chita Rivera: The Dancer's Life, Fosse, Urinetown, Hairspray,* and *Nunsense* to name a few. He has served as the musical director of The Radio City Christmas Spectacular in various cities across America, and has conducted the show in New York. He also was privileged to serve for a time as the musical director of *The Fantasticks* during its nearly 42-year original run off Broadway.

As a composer, Gary worked extensively with the New York-based improvisation troupe, Chicago City Limits. He wrote and arranged numerous sketches and songs for them during his six year stint as their musical director. He also composed the incidental music for Broadway's *Avenue Q* (2004 Tony® Award, Best Musical; 2005 GRAMMY® Nomination), for which he served as the original conductor.

His debut musical, *Altar Boyz* (2005 Outer Critics Circle Award, Outstanding Off-Broadway Musical), has been praised by critics and audiences alike. Gary was nominated for two 2005 Drama Desk Awards (along with his collaborator, Michael Patrick Walker) for both music and lyrics. Gary also created the musical world of "Johnny and the Sprites" (starring *Avenue Q*'s John Tartaglia) on the Disney Channel, both serving as its musical director and writing music and lyrics for numerous episodes.

Gary wishes to thank his niece, Abbey Buckley, without whom the inspiration for this musical would never have materialized.

© Carol Rosegg

## MICHAEL PATRICK WALKER

Born in the small town of New Freedom, Pennsylvania, Michael has been playing the piano since the age of 5 and working professionally in the theatre since graduating from Carnegie Mellon University in 1993.

Michael has been both the music director/conductor and associate conductor of *Avenue Q* on Broadway at various times during its run. His other Broadway and off-Broadway credits include the orchestras for *Wicked*, *Thoroughly Modern Millie*, *La Bohème*, *The Lion King*, *Cats*, *The King and I*, *The Fantasticks* and *tick, tick…BOOM!* He also served as the associate conductor on national tours of *Jekyll and Hyde* and *The Scarlet Pimpernel*, as well as on the Ahmanson Theatre's production of *3hree*.

Michael's first professionally-produced musical, *Altar Boyz*, opened off Broadway on March 1, 2005 and was acclaimed by critics and audiences alike. The show was honored with the 2005 Outer Critics Circle Award for Outstanding Off-Broadway Musical and was nominated for a 2005 Lucille Lortel Award for Outstanding Musical. In addition, the show received seven Drama Desk Nominations of which Michael (with his collaborator, Gary Adler) received two – for Outstanding Music and Outstanding Lyrics.

As of January 2007, the New York production of *Altar Boyz* has played over 750 performances and is approaching its second anniversary! Additional companies have toured the United States and had sit-down productions in Detroit, Des Moines and Seoul, South Korea where the show was translated into Korean. More international productions (and translations) are in the works!

Beyond *Altar Boyz*, Michael is a featured composer/lyricist for the Disney Channel series "Johnny and the Sprites," starring Tony® Award nominee John Tartaglia. He is also currently writing several new theatre pieces and developing an original movie musical.

© Carol Rosegg

© Carol Rose

Nick Ruechel photo, courtesy of SpotCo

Andy Karl      Ryan Duncan      Scott Porter      Tyler Maynard      David Josefsberg

| 7 | WE ARE THE ALTAR BOYZ |
|---|---|
| 16 | RHYTHM IN ME |
| 22 | CHURCH RULEZ |
| 28 | THE CALLING |
| 33 | THE MIRACLE SONG |
| 41 | EVERYBODY FITS |
| 46 | SOMETHING ABOUT YOU |
| 51 | BODY MIND & SOUL |
| 59 | LA VIDA ETERNAL |
| 65 | EPIPHANY |
| 72 | NUMBER 918 |
| 80 | I BELIEVE |

© Carol Rosegg

Book by
Kevin Del Aguila

Music and Lyrics by
Gary Adler & Michael Patrick Walker

Conceived by Marc Kessler & Ken Davenport

"THANK HEAVEN FOR ALTAR BOYZ!
It keeps you laughing all evening long.
If laughter is a form of salvation,
then my soul is clean!"

–Howard Kissel, *New York Daily News*

To learn more about ALTAR BOYZ and the other great musicals
available for production through R&H Theatricals,
please visit our award-winning website
**www.rnhtheatricals.com**
or contact

229 W. 28TH ST., 11th FLOOR
NEW YORK, NEW YORK 10001

THEATRICALS

PHONE: (212)564-4000
FAX: (212)268-1245
E-MAIL: theatre@rnh.com

# WE ARE THE ALTAR BOYZ

Words and Music by
GARY ADLER

**Slow and Religious and Frightening**

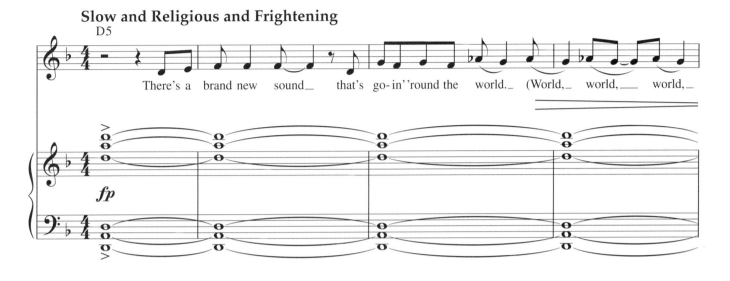

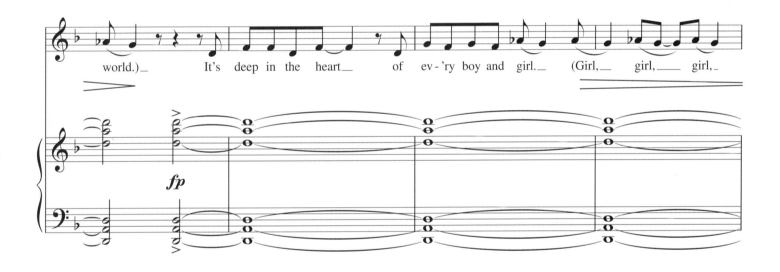

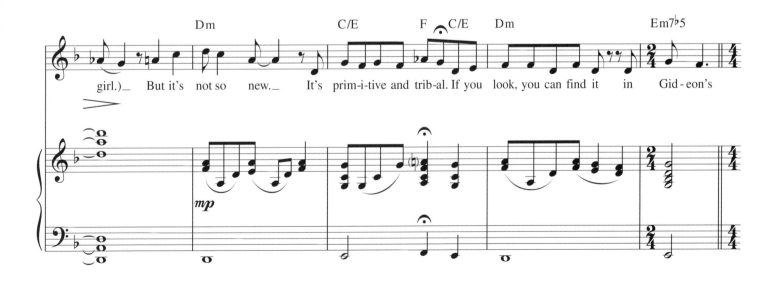

Al - tar Boyz! And we can e-ven name the Saints.__ We are the Al - tar Boyz! We think that

church is su-per fine.__ We are the Al - tar Boyz! We love the wa-fers and the wine.__ We are the

Al - tar Boyz! And I think you'll find_____

We're gon - na al - ter your mind!

# RHYTHM IN ME

Words and Music by
MICHAEL PATRICK WALKER

**Tempo di Funky White Boy** ( ♩ = 132)

# CHURCH RULEZ

Words and Music by
GARY ADLER

# THE CALLING

Words and Music by
GARY ADLER

**Tempo di Verizon** (♩ = 62)

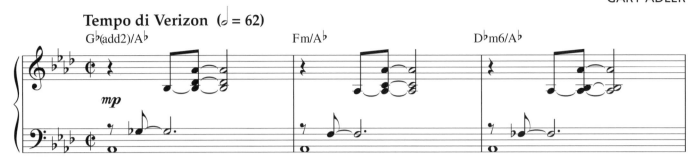

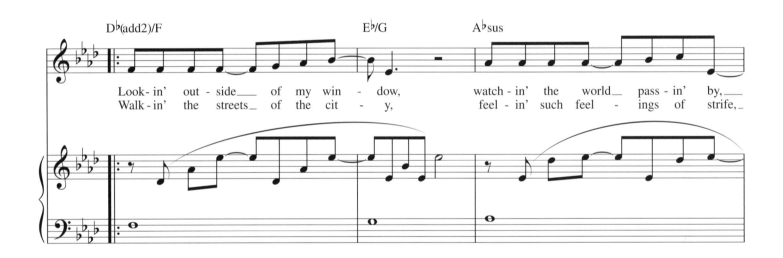

Look- in' out- side___ of my win- dow, watch- in' the world pass- in' by,___
Walk- in' the streets___ of the cit- y, feel- in' such feel- ings of strife,___

___ feel- in' so ter- ri- bly lone- ly,
___ leav- in' my friends___ all be- hind___ me,

# THE MIRACLE SONG

Words and Music by
MICHAEL PATRICK WALKER

**Tempo di Fresh Prince** ( ♩ = 110)

N.C.

John 2:__ Moth-er Mar-y got in-vi-ted to a wed-ding, ev'-ry-bod-y's drink-in', ex-ci-ted, when

all of a sud-den, the wine gave out! Mar-y on the Q. T. gave J. C. a shout.

B♭m    N.C.    B♭m

Je-sus said, "Wom-an, wha-do I have to do with you?" (He was on-ly there to par-ty with his 12 mem-ber crew.) But

N.C.    B♭m    F7♯9(♭13)    N.C.

Mar-y was his mom-ma so he said, "Fill up those pots with wa - ter" and they did think-in' it was worth a shot.

# EVERYBODY FITS

Words and Music by
GARY ADLER

# SOMETHING ABOUT YOU

Words and Music by
GARY ADLER

**With self control** (♩ = 90)

When I met you, girl,___ I knew___ you were___ the
hold your bod - y next___ to mine,___ It

one I'd be___ with all___ my life. And I knew that I'd___ be mak -
feels so good___ and feels___ so right. And it al - so makes___ my Le -

- in' you___ my wife.___ So I hope you'll un - der - stand,___
- vi's feel___ real tight.___ All my friends, they think___ I've lost___

**Slightly slower (♩ = 82)**

# BODY MIND & SOUL

Words and Music by
MICHAEL PATRICK WALKER

# LA VIDA ETERNAL

Words and Music by
GARY ADLER

**Salsa! (♩ = 100)**

You're ly - ing in___ your bed a - wake___ at night,
af - ter - life___ is not___ a scar - y place.

You're safe and warm___ and ev - 'ry - thing's___ al - right.
It's some - thing that___ we all___ one day___ must face.

* Rhymes with "day"
** Rhymes with "go"

# EPIPHANY

Words and Music by
MICHAEL PATRICK WALKER

-ers,    and  your  doc - tors,    and  your  Burg - er  King__ cash - iers!    We're  your  re -

cep - tion-ists,    your  in - terns,    and  your  Am - trak  en - gi-neers!    We  are  your  law -

- yers,    and  your  tour__ guides,    and  your  ac - tors  on__ T.  V.    We  are  your  par -

- ents,    and  your  broth - ers,    and  your  chil - dren,   and  me!__    I  am  a  Cath-

# NUMBER 918

Words and Music by
MICHAEL PATRICK WALKER

# I BELIEVE

Words and Music by
MICHAEL PATRICK WALKER

Gently, in 2 (♩ = 75)

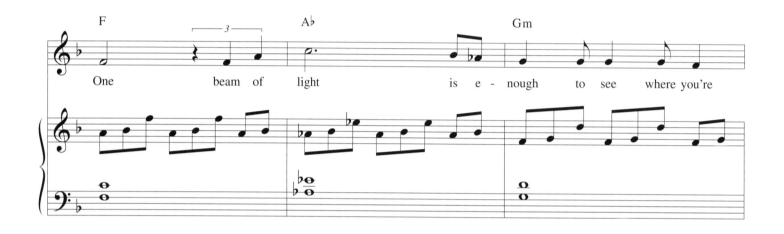

One _____ beam of light is e - nough to see where you're

go - ing. _____

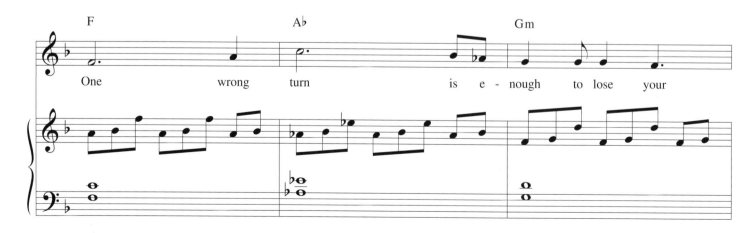

One _____ wrong turn is e - nough to lose your

I___ be - lieve___ that the things that you say___ will come true.___

___ I be - lieve that with___ you in___ my life___ I'll make it.___

_____ I be - lie - ie - ie - ieve_____ in you!___

___ One mis - take___

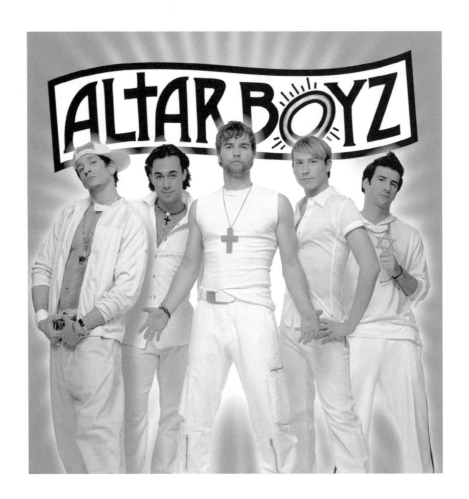